MY WAY TOO

By David P Perlmutter

<u>Copyright © Statement</u>

Published by David P Perlmutter

Edited by Julie Tucker

Other books by David P Perlmutter

WRONG PLACE WRONG TIME

FIVE WEEKS

MY WAY

MY WAY FREE

davidpperlmutter.com

TABLE OF CONTENTS

INTRODUCTION

Hello again, yes it's me, writing another marketing book, sorry it took so long. So following MY WAY, I'd like to welcome you to MY WAY TOO, which I hope you enjoy and from which I hope pick up a book marketing tip or two in order to sell more of your books.

Following the success of my first book WRONG PLACE WRONG TIME, and then MY WAY and FIVE WEEKS, I thought I would write a sequel to MY WAY and in this book I'll tell you how my stories have been received by my audience and also introduce you to a number of the talented authors I've met along the way, together with their books. MY WAY TOO is not to tell you how to market your book, some of my tips I'm sure feature in your marketing plan already, it's just to tell you how I market my books and hopefully my tips can help you?

So let me begin by telling you a bit about my books which are on Amazon!

<u>WRONG PLACE WRONG TIME</u>

#1 BEST SELLER in BIOGRAPHY in the UK!

#1 BEST SELLER in TRUE CRIME in America!

#1 BEST SELLER in TRUE CRIME in Australia!

#1 BEST SELLER in FACTUAL in Spain!

Over 480 reviews on Amazon with 285 being 5* and 85 being 4*!

It's been a couple of years since WRONG PLACE WRONG TIME was published and not long after that I pressed the Amazon self-publishing button for my second book MY WAY. I'm also happy to say that my third book, FIVE WEEKS, has recently been self-published. For those who have not heard of me, and why should you have, let me give you an insight into the books by me, David P Perlmutter, the so called author.

In 2011 I started to write WRONG PLACE WRONG TIME, which to my complete surprise and as you can see above, became a #1 best seller in certain categories across the globe. So let me start by saying that twenty four years ago, I had a terrifying experience when I visited Marbella in Spain and ended up most definitely being in the wrong place at the wrong time. Fifteen years later, while I was living in Portugal,

I thought it would be cathartic to put what happened to me down on paper, I guess it was being overseas that gave me inspiration.

I began to write a blog of my experiences in Spain and after uploading a couple of posts on my blog my friend and former work colleague, Elaine Denning said: *"David, you must carry on with this story, not on your blog but as a book."* And so I did, with Elaine editing the book, as she has worked with many authors around the world and also with help from my brother who designed the cover.

I used Steve Caresser's professional services at ePrintedBooks to format the book and also my other books and since then have recommended him too many authors around the world. In fact he is a great 'INDIE ONE STOP SHOP', as the very talented author Rebecca Scarberry has also stated. I fully recommend ePrintedBooks to all indie authors. Here is Steve's website! www.eprintedbooks.com

To my amazement, as of today, WRONG PLACE WRONG TIME has received over 450 reviews across Amazon with 266 being 5 stars, 75 being 4 stars and around 40 odd are 1 star reviews. Before I clicked the self-publish button, Elaine did warn me that I should be prepared for 1 star reviews and particularly due to the nature of my story some of them would be quite personal and hurtful, and so they were. The names I have been called did hit me hard in the early days soon after the book was available on Amazon.

Yes the book is a true story and I did make some catastrophic, life changing mistakes, so I can in a way understand the readers' opinions, but to be called a scumbag and suggest that I blamed everyone else and that I'm guilty and various other insulting names, did really hurt. Now I take the negative reviews on the chin, I guess I have learned to grow a thicker skin plus the very many 4 and 5 star reviews help to soften the blow.

WRONG PLACE WRONG TIME has been a HUGE surprise to me, not only for the reviews but also the rankings it has achieved in different categories on Amazon across the world, as I have already mentioned. Currently, as of today, the book stands at #1 in biography in the UK. Also since it has been published the book achieved the heady heights of #1 in True Crime in America and also #1 in Australia, and #1 in Factual in Spain, where the events in the book took place. Knowing that I have an international audience that buys my books and then takes time to place a review, whatever star it is, makes it all worthwhile.

David P Perlmutter

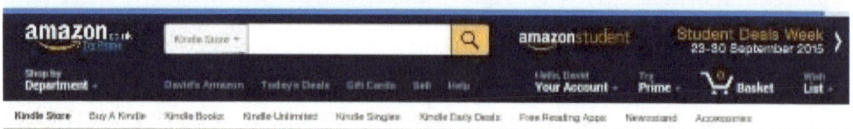

Kindle Store   Buy A Kindle   Kindle Books   Kindle Unlimited   Kindle Singles   Kindle Daily Deals   Free Reading Apps   Newsstand   Accessories

Amazon Best Sellers
Our most popular products based on sales. Updated hourly

Any Department
  Kindle Store
    Books
      Teen & Young Adult
        Biographies
          Cultural Heritage
          Historical
          Literary

Best Sellers in Teen & Young Adult Biographies

Top 100 Paid   Top 100 Free

1

Wrong Place Wrong Time Gripping true...
by David P Perlmutter
★★★★☆ (-) (328)
Kindle Edition
£0.99

2

Wounds of the Father: A True Story of...
by Elizabeth Garson
★★★★★ (-) (23)
Kindle Edition
£1.99

3

Dirty Old Man (A True Story)
by Moll French
★★★★★ (-) (277)
Kindle Edition
£0.99

4

Sunlight on My Shadow
by Judy Liautaud
★★★★★ (-) (14)
Kindle Edition
£7.78

5

Thin Wire: A mother's journey through...
by Christine Lewry
★★★★★ (-) (157)
Kindle Edition
£1.99

6

Bulletproof
by Maci Bookout
★★★★☆ (-) (19)
Kindle Edition
£3.95

7

DEVILS PLAYGROUND

8

Ad feedback

Also I am in the process of having discussions with two film companies who have expressed an interest in making a proposal to me to have my story turned into a film adaption, either on television or on the big screen. I won't hold my breath as the talks have been ongoing for some time, but I guess it's a step in the right direction and yet again further exposure for the book. It's also nice to read in reviews that people do want to see a film made about my story, in fact some reviewers have even mentioned a number of actors to play my role in the story, such as Danny Dyer, Daniel Mays, Marc Warren and even Tom Hardy, which is very flattering.

For those of you who haven't read WRONG PLACE WRONG TIME, I thought I would share a few of the many reviews I've received:

"What a great story! It's been my experience that truth is often more bizarre than fiction. This book demonstrates that point perfectly! "Wrong Place Wrong Time" was a very pleasant surprise. I actually expected the plot to be reasonably interesting. But I hadn't expected the author's style of writing and extremely vivid descriptions to bring me right into the story as if I were there myself. It was very late at night when I began reading this book and I had only intended to read the first couple of chapters. However, once I began, it was impossible to put down. I would not be surprised to see this book be

turned into a movie some day. If it does, I'll be one of the first in line to watch it! While the plot is vaguely reminiscent of "Midnight Express" I found the story to be much more enjoyable. David Perlmutter is a very effective author with a unique style of writing that I will look forward to reading in the future. I have no reservation about giving this book a strong 5 star rating!"

"I really enjoyed this story based on true events! It is quite an adventure for the reader as David's journey into a nightmare moves along quickly from one sticky situation to the next. It shows a lot can happen in a month! David's writing is so easy to read, you are left to enjoy the roller coaster ride which starts with a big mistake! As I read, I could picture everything that was happening so well, I felt I was a fly on the wall watching it, feeling every emotion that David did, from depression and despair to elation and panic, and for this reason, I began to think of it being made into a film. Who would play David? Oh, that's easy - a brilliant actor such as Tom Hardy would be perfect! I can see it all. This is not an idea driven by my own excitement, but of common sense. The sooner someone in the film industry makes David an offer he cannot refuse, the sooner we can all be enjoying it at the cinema and the success of this book can be spread further. Well done David for retracing your steps to the tiniest detail, for being so honest about the negatives as well as the positives that occurred, and for writing it in a wonderfully gripping way!"

"WOW!! I cannot believe how good this book is. If you like True Crime you will love this. I think I have felt every emotion possible reliving the nightmare with David. What an author. I hope and wish to see more from David as his writing style draws you right in until the point you forget what is around you, and instead see everything from his eyes."

"This book was hard to put down. The talented author described Marbella from a traveller's perspective so realistic, I was immediately sucked into the tale and taken back to my own travelling days. From that moment on, I could not stop reading. My heart pounded as I followed the author through his harrowing ordeal *after finding himself in the wrong place at the wrong time, with no apparent way out. A must read, especially for anyone who spent their youth travelling Europe with empty pockets and backpack."*

AUDIOBOOK OF WRONG PLACE WRONG TIME

Another way of spreading the word about your book is to make an audio book and therefore potentially earn further royalties at the same time as well as increase those all important reviews. The audio book of WRONG PLACE WRONG TIME has been a great success so far and it's only been available for five months. I used ACX which is part of Amazon and it was a rather exciting process. First of all you register with ACX then they ask you to put a chapter on your dash board for narrators to contact you with their version of the chapter. I had around twenty who contacted me with their narrative and it was incredible to hear my words being voiced with so many different styles and accents.

There are many reasons why, in the end, I chose Brain J Gill to become the voice of WRONG PLACE WRONG TIME. Namely because of his experience as a narrator of many books and also I quite simply liked the sound of his voice. Even though he is American and the story is based about an Englishman, his English accent was second to none and his voice was so dramatic, something which I felt was required because of the nature of the story.

Also ACX kindly give you FREE codes for the book for you to giveaway in promotions and competitions on your blog, website, Facebook and Twitter. Similarly if another author is arranging a promo you can incorporate your audio book if invited and thankfully I have been invited to many. Through a contact, I have also given away a number of audio books in a competition on an English speaking radio station in Portugal called Kiss FM based in the Algarve. My audio book was featured as a main prize in a competition which ran for a whole three hour Sunday Morning show.

With these FREE codes, you can also have the audio book sent as gifts so why not send one to family members and friends when it's their birthday or even send as presents at Christmas. This is another great way to get your book out there and gain reviews.

Arranging the audio book will not cost you a penny if you go the same route as I did. Yes you can pay the narrator chapter by chapter and once the audio version is complete and available you receive 100% of the royalties, but I opted to share any royalties of the audio books that were sold and therefore no initial outlay. I chose this option at a 60/40 split which has worked out so well. Plus as the narrator wants to earn his split, they will also promote the book so the more audio books sold the more they receive. Really it's a win, win situation for both the author and narrator.

Once the audio book is finished, sit back and listen to your story and I bet you will have goose bumps, believe me, it's a wonderful feeling to hear your story come to life. I am in the process of having my other books turned into audio, following the success of my first. Importantly your Amazon page will look so much more professional when potential readers notice that not only are your books available as a kindle and paperback, but also as an audio book. For a self-published author this for me was something so special. So arrange for your story to become an audio book and hear the words come alive and then market the hell out of it.

Don't hang around, do it authors!

MY WAY

MY WAY, my second book is all about book marketing for the self-published indie author, who hasn't had the advantage of having had an agent or publisher to market their books. However, since I have self-published, I have written to several traditional publishers but each time the door has been gently closed on me. At least they weren't slammed.

I have found that unless you're a celebrity or in exactly the RIGHT PLACE at exactly the RIGHT TIME then it's almost impossible to get an agent, and without an agent it's very difficult to be picked up by a publishing company, and believe me I have tried. In fact I had cocktails with a ghost writer recently who has written for many celebrities and who has said that she will put me in touch with an agent. She has in fact arranged to set up meetings with three agents within the next month, so fingers crossed. As they say it's not what you know, but who you know! And until that time comes when I do or if I get picked up by a mainstream publisher, I am very happy to continue to self-publish and market MY WAY on social media and print, which is something I have a passion for, especially as it doesn't cost me a penny. Only my time. Priceless.

If you have read MY WAY then I hope some of the marketing tips have helped you gain sales and reviews, and you will know what I enjoy doing, and that is promoting myself of course and other authors on social media platforms. As I write, MY WAY has received around 100 reviews across Amazon with 90% being 4 and 5 star reviews, of which the vast majority are from authors. To see some reviews with the headers *"Heaven Sent"*, *"Indie Bible"*, *"Some Twitter sense at last"*, *"I've read MY WAY and now the world is my oyster"* and *"MY WAY is the way."* makes it all worthwhile and it is truly so surprising to me.

I am very proud of the reviews that I have received for MY WAY from authors around the world. I have selected a few of my favourites to share with you.

"In MY WAY David has written a valuable resource for indie authors, showing us his marketing strategies. Too often this type of book is full of hype with little information but not this one. Written in the same style as his book WRONG PLACE WRONG TIME this is a no nonsense look at the hoops indie authors have to jump through to make their voice heard and get their books in front of the reading public. I've been at this for 18 months now and even I learned a thing or two! Thanks for this little gem of a book David, I'm off to implement the holes in my marketing strategy!"

"It was with some trepidation that I approached MY WAY by David

P Perlmutter as, often times this type of `how to' book can leave you feeling more confused and inept than ever. Not so, however, with this one. Perlmutter metaphorically takes you by the hand and leads you through the various sections (Twitter, blogging, Facebook etc.) designed to help you market your book. The premise of the book is that Perlmutter himself is the author of a bestselling book and he is sharing the marketing tools that he used in order to achieve this. The strength of the book lies in the fact that it seems to have been written from the heart. Perlmutter genuinely seems to want to help other writers to achieve the same success and his tone throughout is warm, encouraging and sincere. I came at the book as a technically challenged, marketing disaster and found it incredibly useful. I'm not sure how much success adopting Perlmutter's advice will bring but prior to reading MY WAY I had done only a fraction of the strategies he has recommended. I like the way the book is set out in sections so someone like me, with not much know how, can easily refer back to specific advice. If you struggle to get your head around social media and all things technical then I don't think you can go wrong with this book."

"Everyone knows that indie authors don't get a lot of publicity and if they do, they have to do it all on their own because they don't have an agent or a publicist. If they did, they wouldn't be indie authors. However, just because someone is an indie author, doesn't mean that they will automatically not get the success that they hope to get. They just have to work a little harder in order to get the success by promoting their work. And just how do they do that? Well, David P Perlmutter's book MY WAY is a great guide for them. Of course it isn't the bible for the success of indie authors but from reading it, I say that indie authors will get some great tips from it. I also believe that this isn't just for indie authors. It can also help people who are promoting a small business. What's really great about this instructional book is that it's not a long one. It's short, sweet and gets right to the point."

"To be perfectly honest, I have downloaded improvement books before and quite frankly could not get past the first few pages *without yawning or falling asleep. MY WAY by David P Perlmutter was different. It was interesting from the first page to the last. I found this book very informative, especially if you are a new author looking to get started in the business of selling your books to perspective readers and getting book reviews to help those sales. David goes into detail explaining what market strategies he used to promote his first book WRONG PLACE WRONG TIME which became the #1 bestselling book in 'True Crime' on Amazon in the U.S. in ten short months after it came out. Shortly afterwards it became a #1 bestseller in `Factual' in Spain and #3 in `True Crime' in France. Very recently it became a #2 bestseller in Japan. This book contains no fancy words, just true experience that launched WRONG PLACE WRONG TIME to the 5 star book which it has become. In this book David mentions the importance of blogs, links, websites and even YouTube for promoting your book. The importance of setting the right price for your book is stressed, keeping it low if it is your first book so that it will catch on. He has even had promotions for his eBook listing it as free for a certain period of time. He stresses the importance of places like Twitter to market your book and how important it is to constantly promote your own book. I read constantly and enjoy re-tweeting books for authors, which I follow on Twitter. Sometimes I have to scroll down to get to the book or books the author has written, not David's. I can find it right there on his wall very easily as he constantly promotes it numerous times daily."*

"This book is perfect for those just starting out who want to know how to get started on the road to success. It's just as perfect for those of us who feel like we have already been there and done that, but still haven't reached the kind of sales we'd like. Everyone, whether you are a newbie or a seasoned veteran, needs to take a check every now and then and be honest with yourself as to what works and what doesn't. Warning – David P Perlmutter gives us the steps and tips we need to be successful, but there is no magical potion. It boils down to hard work. That's how you know he's the real deal. No gimmicks, no short cuts, no crazy promises just really good advice from someone who has been there and done it."

"I downloaded MY WAY by David P Perlmutter during a free giveaway, knowing that Mr Perlmutter is always high in the rankings/lists on Amazon. I wanted to see what advice he had to offer to reach such lofty standards. I was very pleasantly surprised.I had read and reviewed Dave's first book, WRONG PLACE WRONG TIME, and enjoyed his easy-going writing. He continues this back porch, sipping iced tea, conversation method of writing in MY WAY.

Simply put: The premise of this book is to explain how to achieve sales and better rankings on the book sales sites such as Amazon. His advice is solid. His explanations are simple, concise, and easy for even the most novice of authors to understand – as a matter of fact, his book should be purchased as a 'handbook' for authors new or seasoned."

"I plan to make very good use of Mr Perlmutter's book. I am including the cover in my power point presentations at my personal appearances to encourage newbie authors to purchase the book for guidance. I certainly wish I'd had something as useful and helpful as this book when I published my first book. I not only highly recommend MY WAY by David P Perlmutter, I suggest that you keep it close at hand as a reference at all times!"

"This book was recommended to me by a fellow author and, if you know me you'll know I'm not much given to superlatives, but it is fantastic! Precise and succinct, it's a complete kit for how to market your self-published book. There is no verbiage, no padding, no unrealistic promises just solid good sense written straight from the heart of someone who knew what he wanted and set out to get it. I have needed a kick up the posterior for some time, to get my marketing going, and when it arrives packaged as a genuinely-written, and often humorous, call-to-action, how can I ignore it?"

"Reading this book, MY WAY by author David P Perlmutter is like having your own enthusiastic professional coach, mentor, advisor, who is solely interested in the publication success of your work! Written for commercial or indie authors, the same promotional

principles apply.

All aspects of using social media, Twitter, FB, other sites, promoting books are covered. The main focus is on networking, and remembering to thank everyone for their interest or help in book promotion. Perlmutter lists pages of people's names who have helped him, very important he insists. He also believes (correctly) that although indie authors work very hard to publish manuscripts, they are undoubtedly worth the higher asking prices, they may not get read/reviewed/noticed due to the price. Readers generally won't pay more money to read a book by an unknown indie author. His marketing strategy has worked exceptionally well, his true crime book: WRONG PLACE WRONG TIME reached the #1 best seller list in both the U.S. and Spain, and #1 in the U.K."

"As an indie book reviewer, I appreciated and agreed with Perlmutter's insight on the importance of good reviews/comments. He advises authors on the "trash review" where a book is unfairly criticized. This is an unfortunate thing when it happens, but must be kept in perspective and not taken seriously. Not all readers will like a book, for whatever reason, no matter how good the book may be. For every bad review Perlmutter receives multiple good to excellent reviews. There are pages of resources and addresses for further reference. This is a value priced Kindle edition, ideal for gifting too ☺"

Above are just some of the many 4 and 5* reviews from authors for MY WAY. So why not nip to Amazon and take a look at other reviews and read the first chapter for free. The chapters in the book are as follows.

"INTRODUCTION" Chapter 1!

"FORMATTING" Chapter 2!

"BOOK COVER" Chapter 3!

"AMAZON PAGES" Chapter 4!

"PRICING" Chapter 5!

"MARKETING" Chapter 6!

"BLOGGING" Chapter 7!

"FACEBOOK" Chapter 8!

"TWITTER" Chapter 9!

"IGNORING THE MOANERS" Chapter 10!

"WHAT ELSE CAN I DO" Chapter 11!

"IS THAT IT" Chapter 12!

Are you tempted to download MY WAY? I hope so and if you do, as always, I hope the marketing tips help you and if so, I would be most grateful for a review, yes those most important reviews.

FIVE WEEKS

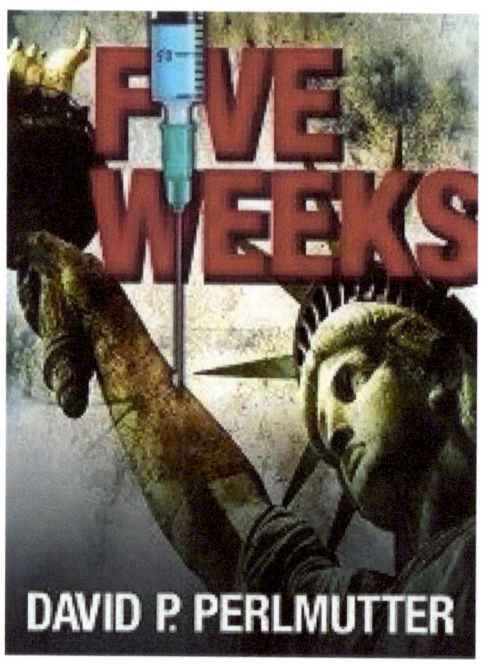

FIVE WEEKS is the story of a British guy who after being involved in circumstances which included having a gun pointed at him, decides to spend a romantic Christmas and New Year by the sea with his girlfriend. After having such a great time, they did decide to move away from London to start a new life together in Brighton. A month later he is offered a job and invited to Altoona in America to train as a Tele-Sales Manager for a well known Portrait Company for FIVE WEEKS. After much discussion, his girlfriend unwillingly agrees that the opportunity before him is too good to miss and off he goes.

With his sales and team building abilities he initially impresses his new manager Michael, whom, it turns out, is a cocaine addict and a drunk, with a Jekyll and Hyde personality. Things take a dramatic turn when he is nearly left for dead in a Pennsylvania forest.

As I have previously said, the book which has recently been released on Amazon has already received a number of 4 and 5* reviews, which are below. Again my brother designed the cover for FIVE WEEKS as he did for WRONG PLACE WRONG TIME, MY WAY and MY WAY TOO!

"Having read the authors first book, WRONG PLACE WRONG TIME which I loved, I had to read this and wow. This is a great story and one yet again I will recommend."

"This is an easy to read book, about an estate agent who due to circumstances leaves London. He lands a job as a Tele-Sales Manager and has to go to America for five weeks of training. The adventure starts for real then. I really enjoyed this well written novel."

"I'm an avid reader of both fiction and non-fiction. However, it's rare for me to encounter a piece of fiction that I enjoy enough to spend the time to write a review. Good fiction, in my opinion, is engaging, reveals something important or interesting about some aspect of the human condition, and – above all – has good story-telling. FIVE WEEKS succeeds in all of these areas. The writing is witty and highly original. Read the first chapter and you'll be hooked."

"Fantastic – recommended. Action comes thick and fast, story moves apace, and great writing."

"Another total page turner. His writing draws you into the story. Thoroughly recommend and can't wait for the next one."

<u>MY WAY TOO</u>

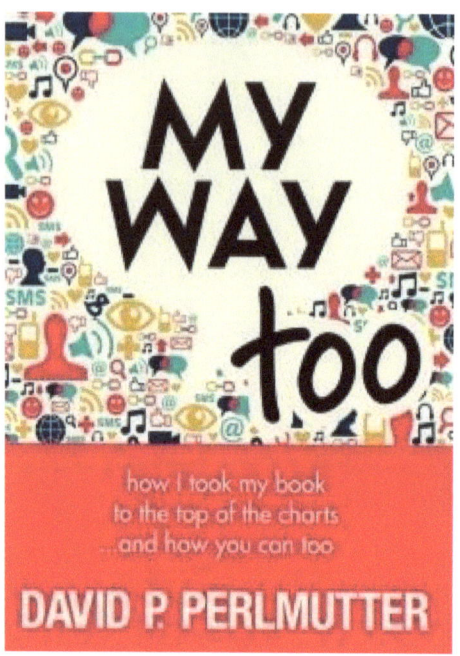

So you may well ask, then again you may not if you are reading this, why I have written another book about marketing?..... Simple! I wanted to show you what has happened since I wrote MY WAY and to inform you of updates relating to my other books. As you have previously read, there have been many, but more importantly, I wanted to see if I could add any additional marketing tips for you to help you in your quest for further book sales and very importantly, receiving those most crucial reviews.

As I have said many times to authors who instruct me to market their books, without reviews you are giving potential readers no guide at all as to whether to take a chance on your book or not. Reviews give people a choice. So with that, let's start the next chapter, which coincidently is all about reviews and opinions.

PERSONAL OPINIONS....

THE GOOD, THE BAD AND THE UGLY!

Hello again and thank you for staying with me.

So reviews. Yes I have already written all about reviews in MY WAY for WRONG PLACE WRONG TIME and other books. As previously mentioned, WRONG PLACE WRONG TIME has received over 450 across Amazon with 266 being 5*'s and they are still coming in. In fact this book has received three further 5* and two 4* reviews within the last couple of days. Isn't that the beauty of eBooks, they will never be put back behind new books as they would be in a bookstore or left behind on the shelf and be lost and forgotten. Once on Amazon, as an eBook, paperback or audio book, they are there for life, unless you un-publish them, that's why continued marketing is so important, and therefore those reviews will not stop coming in and as authors, that's what we want, well, we hope they will continue anyway.

Isn't it so satisfying to know that readers buy our books, they like what we write and leave a review? How is it with you when you see a new review on your Amazon page? With me at the beginning of my journey as an author, my heartbeat increased dramatically and it still does of course when I receive a new one. In the early days when I noticed I had a new review, I used to scroll down the page slowly with anticipation then with bated breath to see what star the review was. That feeling of seeing a new 5* is a wonderful moment, even a 3 or 4* is amazing but there's nothing like a 5* is there?

HOWEVER, when you see a 1*, that dreaded 1*, your heart automatically feels heavy, your stomach begins to do somersaults and it's like the end of the world. Not to mention the knock to your confidence, which for me was soul-destroying. Knowing that someone has read your book, paid for it, didn't like what they read and left a negative review is a horrible feeling to say the least. But you have to move on and remember you just can't please every reader, you just can't. Anyway it keeps it real doesn't it? If you had nothing but 5* reviews for your book then it wouldn't sit right with other potential readers and authors, right? Am I right? I have looked at many books on Amazon and looked at the reviews which have all been 5* and there are many disgruntled reviewers who have put, and I quote, "How can this book have so many 5* reviews, I bet the author got their family and friends to write them." Yes this happens of course, as they are your biggest fans, but every review a 5*? Not even top authors receive all 5*'s. So authors receiving 1/2/3* reviews is not all that bad as long as they are all not 1*'s, yes it may hurt, it may be personal but it keeps it real. Isn't that the beauty of personal opinions?

Of course we market on social media that our book/s have received a 4 or 5* review, well I do anyway, but I also share if I get a 1* review, not everyone admittedly, but the odd 1* that makes me chuckle or if the reviewer has been a nasty name caller. And this 1* review did make me laugh, so I shared it on social media with a link to the book and I'd even included the hash tags for 'Hemingway' and 'Austin Powers' and the response was great. Here is some of that

"Then the main character heads to Spain and I was looking forward to a Hemingway-esque travelogue. What I got instead was Austin Powers on holiday, without even the added tension of Dr. Evil trying to do him harm."

See, I thought this was great and shows that not only does the reviewer have a sense of humour but also the author, which is me! I must say my followers on Twitter loved it. But as you know when we write and self-publish we do leave ourselves wide open to criticism because not every reader will like our style of writing or our story. But hey, you wrote a book so be very proud.

I guess what I'm saying is, these reviews are vitally important so when you get them, tell the world about them across all your social media platforms. Because for every author, no matter how experienced, famous or well published, reviews are what we live for when we write a book, well this is certainly the case for me.

Without doubt it is a massive confidence boost to receive reviews, especially a 5*! Go on check your Amazon page now, and see if you have received one. Also you may have ascertained that I always mention Amazon, or you may not, but to me there is only one website from which readers buy books and that is Amazon. Yes I know there are other book sites, which I have in fact mentioned in a later chapter, but for me it's Amazon all the way. You may disagree and if you do then let me know. It would be great to know your thoughts. I also believe that Amazon should email the author when a new review has been received, or would that be just too much as there are over 4 million eBooks on their site? You tell me authors. I would like to hear your views.

A final note about reviews, I have a word document which has all my reviews, well the decent ones at least and I always add new ones to the list which makes it so much easier and quicker to promote them on social media. So just copy and paste the reviews and tell the world about them.

LONDON BOOK FAIR 2015 & 2016

You may wonder, but then again you may not, why I want to write about the London Book Fair. Well it was the first time I had visited the fair and I wanted to share my views. The event was wall to wall with stands from publishing companies from around the world. Lots of people roaming about and a few authors giving away their paperbacks for free, a couple of which I did take away with me. I also had some great conversations with the authors about marketing and book sales.

In addition there were various seminars by speakers from different publishing companies. The seminar I stayed to listen to was forty five minutes long and it was entitled, "HOW TO SELL YOUR BOOKS." There were some interesting views about how to market your books and social media was top priority, especially Twitter, which I will talk about further in the book. Whilst in the packed arena of this seminar, I stood for the whole time along with two authors I had just met and after having chatted with them for a while, I ascertained that one had just self-published her first book on Amazon and the other had just finished writing her first book. Our conversation soon turned to marketing of course, it's in my blood.

To say I was flabbergasted would be an understatement. Don't get me wrong, I am not claiming to be a connoisseur of marketing, but after asking if they had Twitter accounts, to be told that one didn't have an account at all and the other author never really uses her account as she doesn't understand how it works, I thought, that's my cue!

I must say that despite how it might appear, I'm not a pushy salesman at all, but I just had to tell them that as far as I am concerned, Twitter is a must if you want your book out there, not just in the UK, but worldwide and the best thing about it is..... it's FREE. I also advised them to commence marketing their books immediately even before they became available to readers.

My free advice extended to advising them to put their book covers along with the first chapters as teasers on their blogs which I'm pleased to say they both possessed and therefore gain advanced interest from potential readers. I also suggested to them that they should have a social media book launch to spread the word further and to gain additional attention, feedback and sales, along with receiving those all-important reviews. Let's hope they listened.

Whilst at the book fair I heard one question from an author which was quite interesting, directed to the seminar panel which consisted of four experts in their fields, two bookshop owners, and a representative from a publishing company and a guy from the travel book department of W.H. Smiths. The question was, "I'm a self-published first time author and want to arrange a book tour in my local area and do you have any advice on how to go about this?"

My view on book tours for first time self-published authors is that they are a complete waste of time. Yes I know I may be in the minority here but even the bookstore owners were of the same opinion. As an unknown self-published author without the benefit of an agent or publishing company backing you, it's you who would have to dig deep into your pockets to buy the books, and I'm talking paperbacks, not a kindle version, that you are giving away free. It's you who would have to promote the tour it's you who will have to dig further into your pockets to add any further publicity. What if no one turns up or even just a handful of people? How will that do for your confidence and more importantly to your bank balance. To be honest I haven't tried a book tour. Have you? The only way I would do one is if and when a publishing company signs me; they would promote and market the event as well buying the books. To me, getting your book/s seen by hundreds and thousands, even millions of potential readers is by social media. And it's FREE. Only your time isn't. So my advice, if it's worth anything, don't waste your time OR your money on a book tour. Promote your book first on the many social media platforms out there, gain lots of interest and then once the sales start to happen and money is pouring into your bank account, then think about a book tour, but until then I wouldn't waste your money.

To be quite honest the answers to the questions that were being bounced back and forth, and I must say there were only about five questions, were pretty limited and without wishing to sound conceited, I could have just as easily stood on that stage and given my thoughts about book marketing but in a more detailed, positive and enthusiastic manner, that would have helped the many budding authors in the room to understand how Twitter and other social media platforms can be so beneficial in marketing and selling books.

All in all I did enjoy the book fair and it was worth the £36 entry fee. Will I return next year? I guess you will have to wait for the third instalment of MY WAY which I hope to publish in early 2016. If you are interested in next year's show go to www.londonbookfair.co.uk/ and perhaps I will see you there!

<u>REVISITING TWITTER</u>

I think after the last chapter it's an ideal time to write about Twitter, one of the many social media platforms I use to market my books. People who follow me on Twitter, and as of September 2015 there are over 23,200, (when I wrote 'MY WAY' I had around 12,000), will know I promote my books most days, six out of seven for sure. AND IT WORKS. For me Twitter is the best platform for self-published authors like myself. Yes I use Facebook but it's a different kettle of fish altogether. So sticking with Twitter, I cannot recommend it enough.

If I miss out on a day of tweeting about my books, yes I know there is TweetDeck which enables you to schedule your tweets anytime but there are the odd few occasions that I haven't tweeted for a day or two and I do see the Amazon ranking for my book/s have fallen down the pecking order. I will have a short chapter about TweetDeck later in this book.

As you can see from my Twitter page below, I have an image of my book covers and a professional headshot which my brother photographed. I would recommend that you do the same, as this is what people around the world on Twitter will see first. So catch their eye, because as they say, first impressions count.

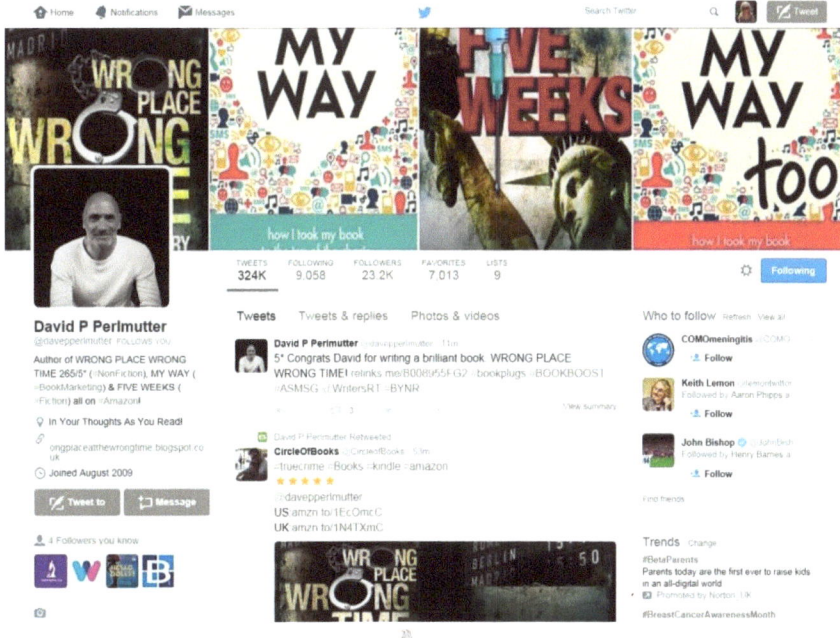

As I have said, if I haven't tweeted for twenty four hours or so then there is a noticeable drop in my Amazon rankings but conversely, after a twenty four hour period of tweeting, I notice my books have climbed back up the all important Amazon charts. This isn't just a coincidence, every time I market my books on Twitter my sales go up and therefore the rankings are higher and furthermore the potential for further reviews increases. It's a no brainer!

TWITTER DO'S AND DON'TS

So getting back to the previous chapter where I talked about the authors I met at the book fair, where one author hadn't t even set up a Twitter account and the other didn't use it through lack of experience, my advice is simple.....

1.   Do set up a Twitter account
2.   Do familiarise yourself with it ASAP and start using it immediately
3.   Do follow people who are relevant

4.   Do follow people who aren't so relevant as you never know who will find you and your book interesting

5.   Do start tweeting about your book but not just about your book!

6.   Do tweet promotions and special offers

7.   Do tweet regularly, minimum three to four times per day

8.   Do spread your tweets throughout the day and night

9.   Do use a decent photograph for your profile pic

10.   Do ask for advice, get in to a conversation and you might find the information valuable

I'm not saying just promote your books and by the way, here are some suggestions (just my opinion) for things to never do on Twitter:

1.   Don't over tweet "buy my book" just don't.

2.   Don't DM (direct message) new followers thanking them for the follow

3.   Don't DM new followers to buy your book or to like your Facebook page, it's insulting and bad manners, and you will lose that follower and a potential reader.

4.   Don't DM people to ask them to review your book

5.   Don't DM people to ask them to download your free book

6.   Don't DM personal messages to people unless you have already established an online relationship with

7.   Don't tweet excessively

8.   Don't just self promote – be sure to promote your fellow indie authors

9.   Don't just auto-tweet – keep your tweets organic

10.   Don't beg

Engage with your followers, keep them interested in you, include a few holiday snaps, photos of family, pets and anything else you wish to tweet, these shared experiences give you the opportunity to interact with current and new followers. It's not all about book promotion and sharing different experiences with your followers, as well as chatting generally about current affairs, may just give them the incentive to download your book.

Also simply ask what your followers are doing for the weekend. Make sure to reply positively to relevant responses. And don't forget that every Friday its #FF (Follow Friday) so tweet your followers with this hash tag and you will gain more followers, just like on a Wednesday with #WW (Writers Wednesday), there are so many ways to gain new followers. It works, trust me!

The channels for telling the world about your book/s are multiple. Why not tweet the cover of your book, get some feedback, ask if your followers like it, start a discussion. It's another way of getting your books out there. Sorry to keep repeating myself but you should, always tweet your 4 and 5* reviews, remember its 140 characters and you will definitely want to add some hashtags within the tweet. The next chapter is all about #hashtags, which you should implement in marketing your books.

I also recommend that you upload the first chapter of your book and book cover on to your website or blog with a link to your book on Amazon and other any other book sites from which your book can be downloaded or purchased, gain interest and comments, again it's all about interacting. Also don't forget to add the Twitter follow icon on your website or blog, or both and do the same with Facebook, Google Plus and other social media platforms you may be with.

Also a picture is worth a thousand words (characters) and photos on Twitter can receive more than twice the engagement, so use them whenever appropriate to show your followers what you're up to, what you have done, and what you may be doing, just continue engaging with your followers.

Also what is great about interaction on Twitter is that when people read your book, some may comment on Twitter saying how much they enjoyed reading the book, or how they like the cover. This again is fantastic publicity for us indie authors and don't forget to RETWEET and more importantly, thank the author of the tweet. Follow them too and I'm sure they will repeat the tweet on a regular basis.

I won't go on about Twitter too much as I did feature it in MY WAY, so why not nip to Amazon and take a look at that book as well and when you're there, check out the reviews from authors who have found it to be an invaluable resource.

If you wish to be one of my 23,200+ Twitter followers then connect with me **@davepperlmutter**

HASHTAGS

In order to maximise a tweet's retweet potential, i.e. for your followers to retweet your tweet to their followers, so causing a domino effect, it is essential to use relevant hashtags to gain even more exposure. So for instance, when you are tweeting about your book, use some of the relevant hashtags which I have listed below. I use them all the time and they do work.

#BOOKPLUGS	#INDIEBOOKSBESEEN
#BOOKBOOST	#BEEZEEBOOKS
#IARTG	#SPSHOW
#BYNR	#WRITERSRT
#RRBC	#eBooksGOT
#ASMSG	#INDIESUPPORT

Also as mentioned don't forget these hashtags for Wednesday and Friday, it will help gain more followers for you, therefore potential readers of your books.

#WW (Writers Wednesday)   #FF (Follow Friday)

And don't forget to also use these hashtags below that could be relevant to the genre of your book.

#NONFICTION	#AMAZON
#ROMANCE	#KINDLE
#ADVENTURE	#EBOOK
#TRUESTORY	#PAPERBACK
#TRUECRIME	#BOOK
#BIOGRAPHY	#AUDIOBOOK
#FANTASY	#BARNESANDNOBLE
#FICTION	#GOODREADS
#EROTIC	#SMASHWORDS

And if you are having a free KDP (Kindle Direct Publishing) promotion, add #FREE within the tweet and for how ever many days the promotion is for, up to a total of five days at your discretion during each 90 day enrolment period in KDP Select, and of course mention the name of the book, with the link.

There are so many ways that you can use hashtags within the 140 characters of your tweet. The more hashtags you use the many more times your tweet will be retweeted.

Also of course don't forget to leave a link to your books for potential readers to click onto and potentially to download your book. If you are promoting the books on your website or blog, again don't forget the leave a link. Yes it sounds like common sense but I thought I would just add it in.

Also retweet as many of your follower's tweets as well. The more support you give, the more support you will receive back and we self-published authors need as much support as possible.

Check out what is TRENDING on Twitter in your country and worldwide and try to incorporate that in a promotional tweet for your book or even just tweet your thoughts about what is trending and you will receive interest from people that you are not already in contact with. Remember most people read so the more you tweet about your book/s the wider your audience will grow and therefore the more followers you will gain and subsequently more potential readers and hopefully more reviews. Makes sense doesn't it?

TWEETDECK

I did say earlier that I would mention TweetDeck, I also mentioned it in MY WAY, but here is a quick reminder. TweetDeck is the most powerful Twitter tool for real-time tracking, organising and engagement and it is what I use to schedule my tweets. What do I mean by this? Of course the world is on a different time zone so when we are asleep, there are parts of the world which are wide awake, so I use TweetDeck to schedule my tweets when I'm asleep. Yes I know it takes up a lot of your time but no one else is going to do it for you and it's FREE. It's your product that you are marketing, so an hour a day to schedule your tweets shouldn't be a major issue. You could always use my inexpensive services if you haven't got time, anyway, if you want potential readers for your books to come from America, Canada, India, Australia, go to Google, put in TweetDeck, sign up and get your product out there for the world to see.

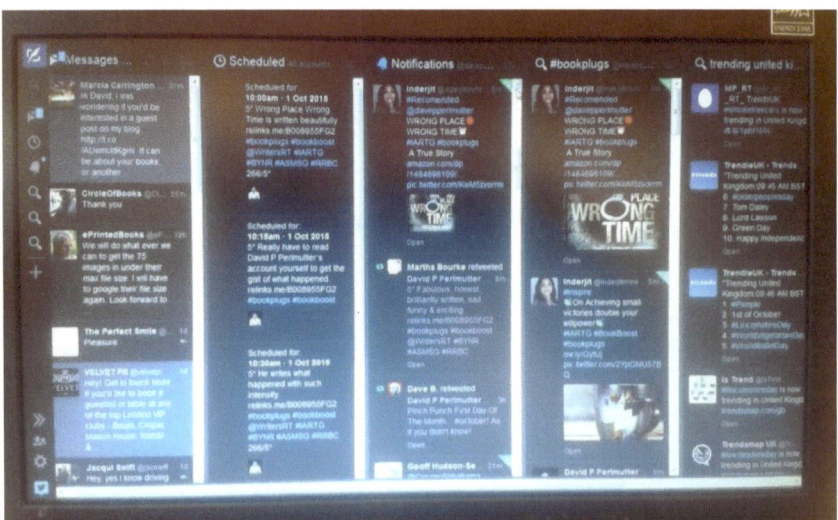

Also with TweetDeck you can add and change columns of your choice at any time, mine are mainly book accounts, like #BOOKPLUGS, #IARTG, #RRBC @WritersRT (in order to see their tweets and retweet them and therefore you can reciprocate their support). As I have already mentioned, you can also check your notifications, your direct messages and also see what is trending at that time and so utilise whatever is trending within one of your tweets to gain further exposure to potential readers. You can also add images, so get your book cover out there. Once again I did mention TweetDeck and other marketing tips in MY WAY, so it may be worth you checking out that book too.

LINKEDIN

I didn't feature LinkedIn in MY WAY because at that time I didn't really focus strongly on this particular platform, but now I do and take my word for it, you must do the same.

Not so long ago I was told by a very good friend to move my butt, update my profile and start working my marketing magic and I am so very pleased I listened. Within a month of pulling my finger out, my number of contacts increased from 150 to over 1500 and my ranking for profile views has shot up their charts.

Of course I market my books on LinkedIn including links plus adding my book cover images but there is also so much more you can do. As you may or may not know I market authors from around the world on all social media platforms and I also offer my services on LinkedIn. I'm delighted to say that due to my improved LinkedIn profile and subsequent activity, I have had many authors contact me directly to take advantage of my book marketing services.

LinkedIn is also a great place to meet and interact with fellow authors and writers, but it's more than that, you can connect with people from all walks of business across all sectors, people you have previously worked with, recruitment agents, existing colleagues, clients, providers, the possibilities are endless. It really is to business networking what Facebook is to social networking, equally powerful and, as I was quick to learn, extremely advantageous. .

It is important to make sure that your profile is updated on a regular basis with a detailed bio to gain interest from fellow followers and importantly a professional headshot, as I have previously mentioned and I can highly recommend Headshots for Business in the UK....

I suggest also that is worth making random updates to your profile a couple of times a week and make sure that you select the 'Notify your network' option so profile change updates get published to your network, so keeping you at the forefront of their minds and adding another opportunity for people to view your profile and/or connect. Additionally do take some time to go through the posts and comments from people on your news feed and you can 'Like' each post that interests you or share it with your own network if you think it will be enjoyed by others. Why not leave a comment? Interacting is so important and do remember it's not all about 'buy my book'!

Another benefit to being on LinkedIn is if you have a meeting planned with someone you haven't met before, or indeed an interview you can search for them on LinkedIn and see if you have any mutual contacts or look for other means of breaking the ice, for example you might notice that they attended the same university as one of your family members or they used to work for a company you had links with. It is always worth doing your homework in advance of an important meeting or interview and as people can see that you have viewed their profile they will appreciate the fact that you have taken time to look them up and do your research, it shows commitment, foresight and professionalism.

There is a facility to request references/testimonials (which you are able to approve before publishing) from former colleagues which enhance your profile enormously and for every category you select as appropriate to your skills such as marketing, advertising, social media, blogging, the list is endless, contacts are able to recommend you.

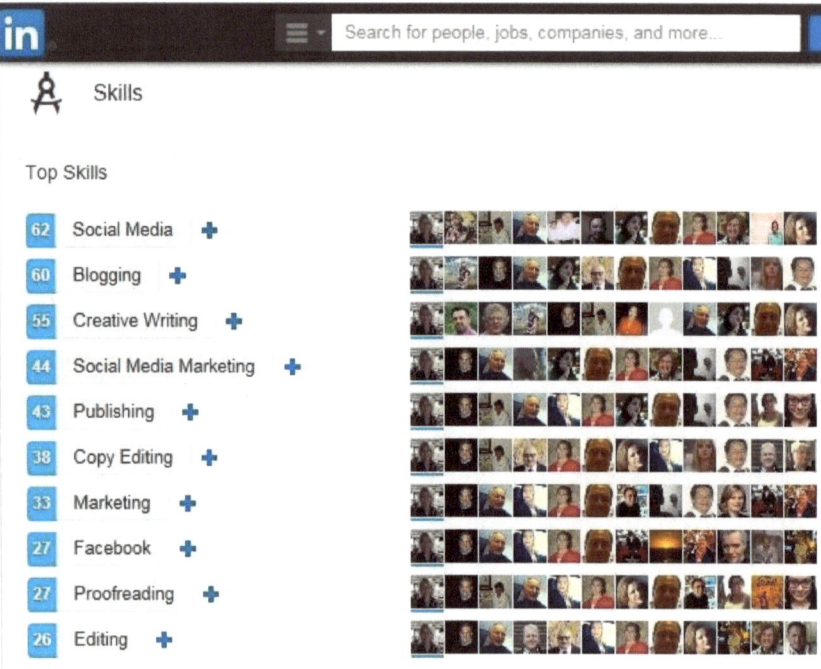

Additionally, particularly appropriate for us indie authors is the opportunity to publish short articles/stories on LinkedIn Pulse. Pulse is an award-winning application that makes it easy to consume business news on mobile phones and tablets. Pulse has been named to the Apple's App Store Hall of Fame, chosen as an Android Editor's Choice app, selected as one of Times's top 50 iPhone apps, and honoured with the Apple Design Award. The company was acquired by LinkedIn in 2013, and incorporated into their own platform.

Oh and yet again, this platform is FREE, unless you wish to subscribe to their Premium service which offers more in-depth use of the product, but I find that the standard free option is quite sufficient for my needs and should be for yours too. You have nothing to lose and everything to gain.

Why not connect, here is my link.

www.linkedin.com/davidpperlmutter

PINTEREST AND INSTAGRAM

Like LinkedIn I didn't mention Pinterest or Instagram in MY WAY as I wasn't an avid user of these social media platforms before but again I most certainly am now and they are both another fantastic way to get your book out there.

Pinterest and Instagram are both free, yes FREE again, where you can upload, save, sort and manage your images and for you authors out there, they are a great visual book marketing tool, so therefore another great platform on which to pin your book covers along with the link to where potential readers can buy your book/s.

With Pinterest, a "pin" is an image that has either been uploaded or linked from a website. Once you have created your boards then you can add pins and other users can *'repin'*, meaning they can *pin* one of your images to their board as well. You can also describe the pin and share it via Twitter or Facebook to all your followers. It is a similar process with Instagram as well.

So authors if you haven't done so as yet, create your accounts and start uploading your book covers ASAP.

BLOGTALKRADIO

Another way of getting exposure for you and your books is being interviewed on BlogTalkRadio. I have had the pleasure of having been interviewed a number of times. There is always great banter and conversation when discussing books, but it's more than that. When I have been interviewed it's not just about books and writing and where I got the inspiration to write, we also talk about the world and life in general. I have added below a link to the radio interview I have done with author and host Janice Ross. I hope you enjoy the repartee.

BlogTalkRadio is based in America and it's the largest blog radio station in the world and so therefore a vast audience of potential of readers who may want to download your book/s. Janice is also an author so she knows the right questions to ask. I had such fun and I fully recommend you do the same.

I met Janice on Twitter so another reason why to have a Twitter account, because you just don't know who you will be in contact with and how potentially you can get the word out there about you and your books.

Also you can join in and have your own blog radio show if you want. So get out there and be part of the largest blog radio station in the world. I have also recently been interviewed via Podcast which a little chapter is dedicated to this later in the book.

<u>CHEEKY MARKETING</u>

I love a bit of cheeky marketing, as my followers on social media will know and I also love a bit of out of the box marketing, it's only a bit of fun BUT it works. It really does.

So what sort of cheeky marketing have I done in the past? Well, with a paperback of WRONG PLACE WRONG TIME firmly in my palm, I visited my local Tesco superstore and placed the paperback in the top twenty bestsellers shelf next to some high profile authors and celebrities, which included the newly released autobiography of Sir Alex Ferguson and the worldwide bestseller Gone Girl by Gillian Flynn. So once I had placed WRONG PLACE WRONG TIME on the shelf between these books, I took a photo and posted the image on all my social media platforms. When I did tweet about it on Twitter, I added @Tesco in the tweet and they retweeted to their many thousands of followers and they even replied adding the hashtag #fergietime.

So you see, *Every little* bit of marketing *helps* !

So at least there was some interaction, also the tweet was retweeted many times by my followers and by adding some of the hashtags that I mentioned before, the tweet was retweeted by them for further exposure. As I keep saying, it's just like a domino effect.

In fact leaving the book WRONG PLACE WRONG TIME on the shelves at Tesco's really worked because my sister went shopping there later that day and phoned me from there to say that she was looking for a book for a friend's birthday present and she saw my book there, which of course I had left. We did giggle and so that's the power of marketing. Out of the box marketing! I actually posted the image only yesterday on Facebook and one fellow author asked if he can take advantage and do the same. Of course I said yes and later in the day he also posted an image of his book on a supermarket's bookshelf. We all have to help each other in this world.

Another way of marketing, and the next example is very cheeky but again it's all in good fun, is to have some chutzpah! (A Yiddish word for confidence and front).

Once when I was at my local pub I asked two very nice couples if they minded posing with my book in their hands and they happily agreed. So a few photos later I had some great shots which I have used as marketing material. There's nothing wrong in out of the box marketing and it's great to see your paperback in someone else's hands with a smile on their face, so try to remember and take a paperback copy of your book/s wherever you go, I know it's not possible all the time but you never know when you might bump into someone who could have an impact if photographed with your book.

For example, a few weeks ago I was in Waitrose in Harrow Weald when I noticed the actor Michael Praed in one of the frozen aisles, presumably buying some Sharwood ready meals and Black Forest Gateaux, (as he is well known for playing Robin Hood in the popular 1980s TV show Robin of Sherwood). In fact Michael Praed is actually mentioned in my book WRONG PLACE WRONG TIME because people used to say I looked like him, when I had a full head of hair! I approached him and told him that he was featured in my book and would he mind having a photo taken with me. He was actually excited and on the spot he googled me, then found my book on Amazon and bought it straight away. Now if I had actually had a physical copy of the book on me that would have added so much more to the photo.

Even still, I tweeted our meeting and included @Waitrose in the tweet. Within a couple of hours I was contacted via Twitter by a freelance journalist Jon Horsley, who writes for

The Sun in addition to the supermarket's own free paper, Waitrose Weekend. Jon wanted to know more about my tweet for a feature he writes called 'The story behind the tweet'.

I responded to say that the story behind the tweet was actually a published book and that I would be delighted to give him further info, so a phone call was arranged for later that day and 9 days later the following appeared on Page 2 of Waitrose Weekend which is given free to customers across its 200+ stores with a distribution of around 400,000 copies.

The story behind the tweet

140 characters explained in 140 words

The tweet So as @MichaelPraed was in @waitrose and as he is featured in Wrong Place Wrong Time had to take a photo. Cool guy.

David P Perlmutter
@davepperlmutter   ⟳ Follow

The story 'I'm a writer,' explains David Perlmutter. 'I've written a book about my life called *Wrong Place Wrong Time*, and it has done very well on Amazon. In fact it was number one in the true crime biography section. In it I mention that, in my younger life, I used to get compared to Michael Praed all the time – he shot to fame as Robin in the TV show *Robin Of Sherwood* during the 1980s.

'I was walking through Waitrose in Harrow,' continues Perlmutter. 'And I saw him doing his shopping. I thought I couldn't miss the chance, so I went up and told him about the book. He posed for a photo, and I told him I'd put it on Twitter, but he said he didn't really understand Twitter. Lovely man, though. Really. And all great marketing for my book.'

Follow @Waitrose on Twitter

And the cheeky marketing didn't stop there. Immediately capturing an image of the published feature, I got straight on to Twitter, Facebook, LinkedIn, Pinterest etc., to promote the article and maximise the marketing opportunity generated by my initial chutzpah at approaching Michael Praed in the first place.

Also featured in the Waitrose Weekend newspaper were contributing editors Philip Schofield, Clare Balding, Alan Titchmarsh, Jonathan Agnew, Jenny Eclair, Paul Gambaccini and others who I tagged in to my tweets along with Waitrose itself, and on Facebook too.

And all this from a chance meeting in the supermarket!

Another cheeky marketing tip is to donate a few paperbacks of your book/s to a local charity shop; they will place them on their shelves, so further exposure and for potential readers to buy. I happened to choose a Cancer Research UK shop, which is down to my editor Julie Tucker who is a Cancer Campaigns Ambassador for the charity. I am currently in the process of becoming an Ambassador for CRUK myself as I have been so inspired by the work they do and also in memory of father, Morris, who passed away from this terrible disease.

Also take a photo of your book/s on the shelf, with permission of course and put the image on all your social media platforms. I did this too and they put the book, WRONG PLACE WRONG TIME in-between Fifty Shades of Grey and One Day, it was a great photo and yes, I marketed the hell out of it. So get down to your local supermarket and charity shops and market away. No one else is going to do it for you.

 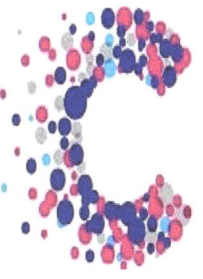

I have to add that I received a tweet recently from a Twitter follower in California to say that she had a garage sale and she sold a paperback version of WRONG PLACE WRONG TIME, of course only after she had already read it and given it a 5* review on Amazon. It's crazy really, here I am in a small village in the UK and one of my books is being offered in a garage sale in the good old US of A.

I also visited a local WH Smith armed with a paperback copy of WRONG PLACE WRONG TIME and cheekily placed the book on one of the shelves, and yes I placed it in the #1 bestseller spot, as you can see from the image. Oh and yes, I did leave the book there too! I'm also pleased to announce that the book is now featured on their book site, the link is below! Add image

Finally a last bit of very cheeky marketing, which I couldn't resist whilst waiting for my daughter to finally come out after a One Direction concert at Wembley Stadium in London last year! So I took this photo standing on a bridge of the wave after wave of people leaving the concert. Straight away I tweeted the image with a message saying, "Great response for my book signing tour, take a look at the queue!" It received many RT's and comments! Of course I posted it on my two Facebook pages, my blog, and all the other social media platforms that I have mentioned in this book.

See, there is no harm in being cheeky!

Oh and according to my daughter the boys were great!

BLOGS AND BLOGS

Another way to receive exposure is being interviewed and featured on blogs from other authors and also for them to read and place a review of your books on their blogs too. Again it's a no brainer and also its great fun, it really is. Not only can you promote your interviews on your social media platforms to give you another way to promote your book/s to gain followers, potential readers, sales and those all so important reviews, but it's also a great way to make friends, well at least on-line anyway. Plus you're also promoting the blog of the author who kindly invited you to appear on their blog. Once again, a win-win formula.

Just to add that recently I have been invited by fellow author Effrosyni Moschoudi for a question and answer interview on her blog. It will be available late October at effrosyniwrites.com

So, below is a list of blogs links that I have been featured in and I want to publicly thank each and every one of you for the invite.

http://www.blogtalkradio.com/

http://bookhippo.uk

http://carternovels.com/

http://electagraham.com/

http://www.greatbooksgreatdeals.com/

http://iamchristianleaf.wix.com/

http://kjwatersauthor.blogspot.com/

http://mrc-bookreviewer.blogspot.co.uk/

http://readersgazette.com/

http://richardfholmes.org/

http://www.rickiwilson.com/

http://ruthjacobs.co.uk/

http://scarberryfieldsforever.blogspot.co.uk/

http://taraford.weebly.com/

http://beezeebooks.com/

http://www.conniesbrother.blogspot.co.uk/

I hope that you can see, by clicking on the above links, how very powerful it is to be invited and to be asked questions about you and your books. Also your interviews are then on the author's blogs for life, so you can continue promoting the interview on a regular basis. Another win-win situation. It is the same with my blog, I have featured many authors from around the world on my blog, and written a chapter about this further on in this book.

BOOK WEBSITES

Below are a few book websites on which I have placed a couple of my books and I would fully recommend that you do the same. Once again some are FREE and some charge a very small fee but it is well worth it. There are many more book websites you can use, but these sites below have been instrumental in my book sales and in gaining reviews, so I thought I would plug them and also introduce them to you. Another win-win situation. It's all about trying to win!

WISE GREY OWL! With 447,500 book views to date and over 8,000 average page impressions per day, I placed WRONG PLACE WRONG TIME on this particular book website and the feedback has been amazing with over 2,000 views of my book. I have recommended this site to many authors around the world and they have taken my advice and placed their books on this site. So if you haven't as yet, do it. Oh and the beauty of this site?....... It's FREE!

www.wisegreyowl.co.uk

ASKDAVID! Incidentally this has nothing to do with me, but it is another brilliant website where you can promote your book/s and yet again it's FREE. The advantage of this site is that they will also tweet your book/s to their many thousands of followers, which is over 42,000 on Twitter and they will give you the opportunity to tweet your book/s directly from their website. So authors don't hang around and ASKDAVID.

http://askdavid.com/reviews/book/true-crime/2002

GOODREADS! This book site will not be new to many authors around the world as this website is an Amazon company. Goodreads is the world's largest site for readers and book recommendations. A few numbers that will make you think. Goodreads have 40 million members, 1.1 billion books added and 43 million reviews. I have my three books on here (with this book soon to follow) and I'm delighted with the number of reviews and ratings I have for WRONG PLACE WRONG TIME, MY WAY and FIVE WEEKS. So once again authors stick your books on here to gain massive exposure and again people, it's FREE!

https://www.goodreads.com/author/show/6333276.David_P_Perlmutter

BARNESANDNOBLE! Barnes and Noble is the largest retail bookseller in the United States, and a leading retailer of content, digital media and educational products in the country. The company operates 658 retail stores in all 50 US states, in addition to 714 college bookstores that serve over 5 million students and more than 250,000 faculty members across the country. So what I'm saying here people, unless you have done so already, get your book/s on here now. It's FREE!

http://www.barnesandnoble.com

SMASHWORDS! Smashwords is a self-serve publishing service. Authors and independent publishers upload their manuscripts as Microsoft Word files to the Smashwords service, which converts the files into multiple eBook formats for reading on various eBook reading devices. Once published, the books are made available for sale online at a price set by the author or indie publisher. Another fantastic FREE site to get your books noticed and to sell, therefore making money. Also another great place where you will receive reviews, as indeed have I.

http://www.smashwords.com/

SELF PUBLISHERS SHOWCASE! SPS is a book website that highlights the best independent publications in fiction and non-fiction. I have MY WAY and WRONG PLACE WRONG TIME on their site and they tweet the books to the 154k plus followers they have on Twitter.

As their website states, they are incredibly fortunate to have amassed over 400 of the finest self-published and small press published authors.

To check out all their authors and my page, please click the link below!

http://selfpublishersshowcase.com/

LOOK 4 BOOKS! Gary Walker is the mastermind behind this book site and he works non-stop to give your books huge exposure! Books that are featured on Look 4 Books, will receive three book promotion posters designed by Gary, mine are below and 365 days a year marketing on social media, and all this for less than £1 a week. For more information contact Gary on Twitter @Gary_R_Walker and check out his Facebook page, https://www.facebook.com/freebookpromotion, where he also promotes all the authors who have their books on his site.

http://www.look4books.co.uk/

Back To Homepage
Have You
Bookmarked Us Yet!

READERS GAZETTE! Is another free website designed to give indie authors better coverage in the book world. They work tirelessly in marketing and promoting the authors, like myself who are on their website with book covers, description and links. It also features quizzes, games, blogs and short stories

http://readersgazette.com

CIRCLE OF BOOKS! Circle of Books is a cracking website promoting many books from indie authors, including a huge range of genres! So why not take a look and add your book! They market books and authors on most social media platforms. They also designed this image for my book MY WAY! The link to their site is below!

http://circleofbooks.com/

RUKIA PUBLISHING! Rukia Publishing - where authors can access support and information on self-publishing book promotion and readers can access information and links to great books in all genres. **Readers looking for good quality, independently published books in all genres are helping Rukia to promote authors. If you read Indie books and would like to get involved please contact Sarah Jane Butfield, Margaret Daly or Shontae Brewster**

www.rukiapublishing.com

author*graph*

AUTHORGRAPH! Authors, have you had any requests for a signed kindle book and thought how do I do that? Well now you can with Authorgraph. I have done many for readers of my books around the world and yes, it's another great way to spread the word about your books. They make it possible for authors to sign their e-books for their readers and fans. Really, it is so simple, even I managed to work it out and the best thing about it, it's FREE!

So what are you waiting for? It takes a couple of minutes to add your book/s to their site, just add your ASIN number and that's it, within a blink of an eye, your book is ready for you to sign. What a great gift this would make. And remember, market the hell out of this amazing opportunity!

For readers who want a signed kindle book from your favourite author, just search or browse for a specific author or for books on the site, click "Request Authorgraph" (you can include a short message to the author). You will receive an email when the author has signed your Authorgraph. You can also view Authorgraph in your favourite reading apps and devices.

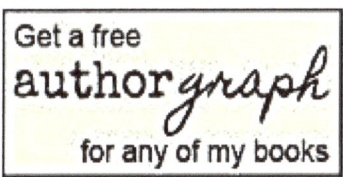

https://www.authorgraph.com/authors/davepperlmutter

Creativia is an independent publisher of exceptional and unique fiction. We firmly believe in indie literature and the new era of versatile publishing. Have a look at some of our author testimonials below, and **learn more about us** and **our services for authors.**

If you're looking for some quality reading, **click here to see our bestsellers.** If you'd like to read any Creativia book for free, **have a look at the Creativia Street Team.**

http://www.creativia.org/

AUTHORS I HAVE FEATURED ON MY BLOG

Now, this is my blog that has received over 72,000 page views and which is viewed throughout the world. Take a look and if you would like your book featured, let me know on Twitter @davepperlmutter

http://thewrongplaceatthewrongtime.blogspot.co.uk/

Ever since I started writing and marketing, there is nothing I enjoy more than supporting fellow indie authors (well there are a few things not suitable to mention here that I do enjoy more, but do look out for a forthcoming title from me which will knock 50 Shades into the dark). I have marketed authors from around the world on Twitter, Facebook, my blog and other social media platforms and I have met many special authors online. Below is a list of very talented authors and their books that I have featured on my blog.

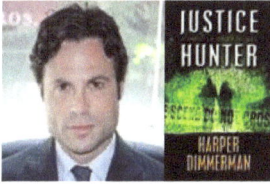

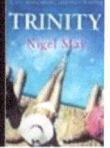

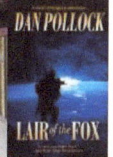

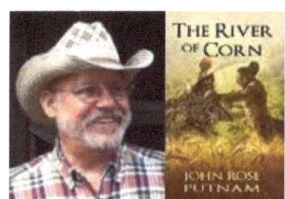

So why not take a trip to my blog and check out the above authors and books.

PODCAST INTERVIEW

Podcast is a digital audio platform and I was kindly invited by K.J. Waters and Suzanne Kelman, AKA Blondie and the Brit, for my first podcast interview which will be live in October 2015. We had a blast discussing books, book marketing tips, some very #cheekymarketing tips and anything else that popped into our heads for the hour long show.

I must say that we didn't stop laughing as the conversation flowed from one end of the world to the other. I can't wait to listen to the interview in full, even though I dislike the sound of my own voice, I do really.

I will be marketing the interview on my blog, Facebook pages and Twitter, so look out for the links and I hope you enjoy the show. And I'm sure you will pick up quite a few marketing tips along the way.

So why not contact KJ and Suzanne, arrange an interview and get podcasting! If you wish to do so, catch the interview and get in touch. KJ and Suzanne can be found on Twitter, @Kamajowa and @suzkelmen.

Also as MY WAY TOO goes to print, or at least the EBook version, Blondie and the Brit are now on iTunes. Each week they will interview an expert in the industry for a fun and informative chat about writing habits, social media strategies, publishing tips, and book marketing advice. Join the quirky

Blondie and the Brit comedy duo for a fabulous adventure in writing, publishing and beyond! Subscribe today so you don't miss a single episode. Visit their website at **www.blondieandbrit.com** for show notes and an upcoming schedule.

YOU TUBE WITH ERIK NELSON

Erik Nelson. What a fine chap he is!

Erik has reviewed many books on You Tube for authors around the world. Erik kindly reviewed MY WAY and the review has so far had over 852 views. Below is the link to the review of MY WAY.

https://www.youtube.com/watch?v=nZWbTm37ifU&sns=fb

I have also featured on my own blog the many reviews Erik has kindly reviewed for many authors and below is a list of the books and authors!

Review for "11/22/63" by Stephen King.

Review for "Always in Tao" by Brian Taylor.

Review for "Amber & Blue" by K.R Rowe.

Review for "Ascent of Blood" by Elizabeth Marx.

Review for "Being There" by Jerzy Kosinski.

Review for "Betrayed" by Wodke Hawkinson.

Review for "Deadly Election" by Arthur Crandon.

Review for "No Easy Day" by Mark Owen.

Review for "The Key Of Amatahns" by Elisabeth Wheatley.

Review for "Killing Kennedy" by Bill O'Reilly.

Review for "Killing Lincoln" by Bill O'Reilly.

Review for "Lake Caerwych" by J.Conrad.

Review for "The Obama Hate Machine" by Bill Press.

Review for "Operation Dark Angel" by Pam Funke.

Review for "Persuasive Lips" by Sherry Silver.

Review for "Return to Rocky Gap" by Toni Wyatt.

Review for "Sexy Stranger Game" by Nikki Hazes.

Review for "The Stolen: Two Short Stories" by Michelle Browne.

Review for "Stiff: Memoirs of a Dick" by Dick O'Connor.

Review for "Summer Winds" by Wanda Smith.

Review for "Tall Dark & Different" by Kimberly Biller.

Review for "Touch Stone for Play" by Sydney Jamesson.

Review for "The Untold History of the United States" by Oliver Stone.

Review for "Username: Bladen" by J.V Carr.

So why not get in touch with Erik who I'm sure will kindly review your book on You Tube. Contact Erik on Twitter! @cluelessbutdumb!

THAT'S ALL FOLKS!

As this chapters says, THAT'S ALL FOLKS so I will say thank you for reading MY WAY TOO and I hope you have picked up a few book marketing tips. If you haven't, then why not take a look at MY WAY, and see if any of the tips in that book may help increase sales.

All I would say is keep marketing your book/s because you deserve for your book to be noticed, read and reviewed.

Good luck my fellow indie authors………

David P Perlmutter